PLAYS, PAGEANTS AND PROGRAMS

FOR

SCHOOLS, CAMPS AND ORGANIZATIONS

by

JOHN R. CARROLL

EDITOR
Frank Alexander

TEXT ARTIST
Dawn Bates

COVER DESIGN
Dawn Bates

Published by FRONT ROW EXPERIENCE, 540 Discovery Bay Blvd., Byron, CA 94514

1,500 BOOKS IN PRINT AS OF 1991

Copyright JOHN R. CARROLL 1990

ISBN
0-915256-29-0

Published

by

FRONT ROW EXPERIENCE
540 Discovery Bay Blvd.
Byron, CA 94514

All rights reserved.
No part of this book may be reproduced in any form or by any means
(except where provided for in the footnote at the bottom of page 1)
without written permission in writing from the publisher.

PLAYS, PAGEANTS AND PROGRAMS
is dedicated to
HAL for his continued support
RUTH for her encouragement
and
MAUREEN for her Tamale Pies

ABOUT THE AUTHOR

John R. Carroll has survived producing, directing and writing dozens of children's plays for schools, recreation departments and camp groups. His involvement in children's theatre includes working for various city recreation departments, teaching creative dramatics to all ages as well as teaching theatre arts at the high school level for several years.

As a published playwright, John has written for adults as well as children and his plays are produced regularly throughout the United States. They include "Oh, What A Tangled Web", "If It Don't Hurt, It Ain't Love", "Murder Well Rehearsed", "The Enchanted Bicycle", and "The Folks Next Door". His educational show "The Marvelous Machine" has toured in schools across the nation and he has written special material for the Los Angeles Music Center On Tour Program which brings the theatre experience to Southern California schools. He has also written several musical comedies including "Babes In Barns" in Chicago and "Ship Shapes" and "Putting It On The Line" which had successful runs in Los Angeles. He free-lances for various magazines and newspapers.

A graduate of Loyola University in Los Angeles, John has done graduate work at Schiller College in London, the University of Nairobi and the American Academy of Dramatic Arts.

CONTENTS

INTRODUCTION ---- 1

THE "WHAT DO YOU MEAN I'M IN CHARGE OF THE SCHOOL PAGEANT?" ---- 2
    PRODUCTION NOTES ---- 3
    CAST LIST ---- 4
    SETTING ---- 5

THE PIED PIPER ---- 22
    PRODUCTION NOTES ---- 23
    CAST LIST ---- 24
    SCENE ONE ---- 25
    SCENE TWO ---- 36
    SCENE THREE ---- 36

THE EMPEROR'S NEW CLOTHES ---- 40
    PRODUCTION NOTES ---- 41
    CAST LIST ---- 42
    SCENE ONE ---- 42
    SCENE TWO ---- 48
    SCENE THREE ---- 52

RED RIDINGHOOD'S ADVENTURE ---- 57
    PRODUCTION NOTES ---- 58
    CAST LIST ---- 59
    SCENE ONE ---- 59
    SCENE TWO ---- 63
    SCENE THREE ---- 65

THE ENCHANTED BEDPOST ---- 70
    PRODUCTION NOTES ---- 71
    CAST LIST ---- 72
    SCENE ONE ---- 73
    SCENE TWO ---- 76
    SCENE THREE ---- 87

INTRODUCTION

Welcome to the world of school pageants. This book, hopefully, will offer you a choice of new plays or pageants that can be personalized to your own school's needs. It sprang from years of trying to find the right plays that were produceable for lower grades. I have tried to give you options to those hokey school plays of the past and have tried to allow room for your own creativity as you direct these plays. These plays are easy to produce and allow each director to shape it to his or her own specific needs. Each play has a cast list that can be cut or added, with optional songs or scenes that will make the show unique to your group alone.

There are no royalties for you to produce these plays.** Included in the book are classic plays like Pied Piper and Red Ridinghood. These have been modernized a bit to add humor and a bit more fun to some old tales. They also, hopefully, have new morals that are as fun as they are timely. These classic plays are about twenty minutes long, depending if music and dance are used. They are good for lower grades from first to fourth. Any older and the kids start really wanting to do "Rambo Meets The Terminator".

The school pageant play and the holiday play are projects for the entire school, using different classes, groups or talent that can rehearse separately from the main body of the work. You can use as much (or as little) talent you can scrounge up. Take advantage of clubs in your schools, such as the choir or band or even the basket ball team. The plays are written so each group is an entity unto itself. Therefore, you, as director, will inform interested teachers or group leaders what their specific group is to learn (song, dance, etc.) and will be able to practice the major dialogue sections while the groups are off rehearsing by themselves.

Each play has a set idea and a few words about costumes as well as directorial guide-lines. It is up to you to use them or not. Remember, these are your shows now and you can be as creative as you want. The sky is the limit (within the school budget, of course).

Putting on a show is not a horribly difficult job. It is fun and rewarding and you should have no trouble using these plays as starting points. They are easy to produce and audiences have enjoyed them when I have directed them for recreation classes.

If the idea of facing thirty pre-pubescent kiddies makes you a bit wobbly, may I suggest you first read a wonderfully clever book that by some coincidence, I have also written, entitled "THE 'WHAT DO YOU MEAN I'M IN CHARGE OF THE SCHOOL PAGEANT?' HANDBOOK" which is available from the publisher, Front Row Experience. It will give you a step by step outline to producing the best pageant your school has ever seen.

Good luck! I'd love to hear how your production went.

JOHN R. CARROLL
P.O. Box 4061
North Hollywood, CA 91607

** Publisher's Note: You have permission to duplicate these plays for use only by your cast and only at your school site or facility. You do not have permission to make copies from this book for other school sites or other facilities in your district or organization. Each separate site or facility needs to purchase its own book for duplication for its own cast. (Each page is perforated for easy removal for duplication.)

THE "WHAT DO YOU MEAN I'M IN CHARGE OF THE SCHOOL PAGEANT?" PAGEANT

PRODUCTION NOTES

This play may sound confusing when you start to read it, but it will make your life so simple that it is worth the extra couple of minutes to make some battle plans before jumping into the fray. It is so simple to produce, if you do your job right.

This play is written to use the talent pool (or some cases, the talent puddle) that abounds in your school. There is one core group of people who handle the dialogue and several groups who come in and do whatever talent you have available. Is there a school chorus? A dance club? A kid who can play the theme from "Phantom Of The Opera" on the saw? Kids who take tap dancing or piano? If so, grab them. Get the club's moderator or another teacher, to work with those groups. This is a perfect framework for a talent show or a P.T.A. group who cannot get everyone to rehearse together for more than a couple of rehearsals.

As the director, you should delegate as much as possible to other teachers or camp leaders while you concentrate on the major sections of dialogue and plot how to get the larger groups on and off the stage. Get a core of teachers to agree to have their class do one small number. (Anyone can do one little number, right?) You may want to leave it up to the individual teacher to decide what talents are smoldering beneath the surface of their own group or make some strong suggestions as to the type of number or scene you'd like to see. You may want to hold auditions for individual as well as group talent. The way this play is set up, each group rehearses separately and come together for only a couple of numbers.

While the teachers are getting their groups into shape, you will be rehearsing the major parts of the play, the dialogue between the director and the other leads. Pick a couple of kids from each class to say the limited lines that are in each group's scene and rehearse with them a couple of times. But for the most part, these groups are self sufficient and will be working with other teachers than yourself. You may feel more like a traffic cop than a director, but you will earn the title by having everyone reporting to you.

You will have to rehearse getting the groups on and off the stage, but it will be easier to let another teacher rehearse and costume their own group. You will also note that there are parts where everyone comes in. This is quite a spectacular bit, since it could be upward to one hundred kids. You'll have to rehearse this so it is orderly chaos. If you choose to have them all do a number, it will require a couple of rehearsals putting the number together. (Hopefully, the teachers in charge of each group has also taught them the group songs.)

You are not limited to the number of specialty acts you do. If you have more classes than there are parts, simply have the "Director" request to see the next group and the next and so on until you have exhausted your pool of talent. Or if you do not have enough groups, eliminate a couple. The play is written to be just as well received with as much talent as you can find.

No talent? Then turn it into a fun "no-talent show" type of play using bad acts...REALLY bad acts that know they are bad can be funny. Roping a couple of parents to do bad comedy routines or sing a golden oldie song from their past (complete with costumes of that era) is charming and funny. Just be sure that the acts you use know they are suppose to be bad and won't be hurt by the laughter of the audience. Remember, the entire concept of the show is that they are not professionals.

The ending number should be pretty snazzy, so you may want to use the best group as the core group, with the others coming in for a big finish.

SETTING
This is played on a bare stage. Yes! No scenery. That is unless you want each group to perform before a flat or two. This can be pretty effective, especially if you are doing, say, songs from Broadway Shows. You might think of having posters of the shows revealed with each group's song and/or dance. At the end of the show, it would be fun to have the back curtains open to reveal a glitzy set with the name of your organization in lights, but the excitement of all those kids singing should be enough.

COSTUMES
Everyday clothes. You might want to have the kids in some type of costume for their individual group numbers or maybe have them all wear cardboard top hats or T-shirts with a star painted on for the finale but again this is supposed to be a rehearsal. The people playing adults should dress more maturely than the others, but again, it is up to you.

MUSIC
Although the play indicates that there are places for songs, you can replace them with recitations, scenes from a drama class, comedy routines or anything that can be deemed talent. You may want to use recorded music or have a pianist to accompany the little darlings as they warble off key. You should know the opening and closing numbers by the time you start so you can have your group leaders teach it to the kids.

CAST LIST

PARTS WITH MAJOR DIALOGUE
(These actors should be the director's responsibility since they are in the scenes between each group.)

>   The Director
>   Veronica Volunteer
>   Mindrot
>   Coach
>   Mr. Sawhorse
>   Pampered Volunteer

PARTS WITH MINOR DIALOGUE
(These characters have one or two lines and are within the specialty groups...singers, dancers, etc. These individuals should have loud speaking voices and the director will have to rehearse with them a few times. But for the most part, they should be the responsibility of the teacher who is doing the specialty groups rehearsal. Their names and gender can be changed depending on your casting and parts can be combined or eliminated per your needs.)

GROUP ONE
Andrea

GROUP TWO
Robby
Carla
Louise
Gerrie

GROUP THREE
Gabe
Chan
Todd

GROUP FOUR
Lenore

ANY GROUP
Ernie
Cindie
Carl
Freddie

THE "WHAT DO YOU MEAN I'M IN CHARGE OF THE SCHOOL PAGEANT?" PAGEANT

------------------------------ SETTING --------------------------------

Your school auditorium or multi purpose room. There are a couple of chairs and tables but for the most part, no scenery.

As the houselights dim, **DIRECTOR ENTERS** from the back of the auditorium. She is burdened down with stacks of scripts and papers and all but drops them on a table when she walks onto the stage. She looks around.

DIRECTOR
Can I get a little more light up here, Stan? And open the curtains, would you? (The lights, if available, come up and the curtain opens. **DIRECTOR** walks around the area.) I wonder if Cecil B. DeMille ever felt like this?

(**VERONICA VOLUNTEER ENTERS**, dressed in a hat and a stole on her way to tea, probably. She is accompanied by her daughter, **PAMPERED**, who wears a frilly dress.)

VERONICA
Oh, there you are, Darling. So good to see you. You look marvelous, just marvelous. (Kiss-Kiss---Her kiss misses Director by a mile.) Well, are we all ready to begin work on this year's school pageant? (To daughter) Pampered, don't bite your nails, dear. It's unladylike.

DIRECTOR
Veronica Volunteer! For once I am glad to see you. I'm going to need all the help I can get on this one. Directing the school pageant is not an easy job. I just wonder how I got stuck with it.

VERONICA
Easy, darling. When I saw that they needed a volunteer to do this year's show, why I nominated you right away. You're the only one who is clever enough. You're the only one who is creative...You were the only one...

DIRECTOR
Who missed the last P.T.A. meeting, I know, I know. Anytime I don't attend, I end up being a chairperson on some committee. I still have a garage full of Junior Chipmunk Cookies.

VERONICA
Well, I am sure you are going to make this year's show memorable.

DIRECTOR
Well, we'll try. Now, I am going to need you to help me decide which show we should do.

VERONICA
Oh, darling, I have a splendid idea...Why not do "Goldilocks"? (She starts brushing her daughter's YELLOW hair.) Hold still, dear, and let mommy brush your hair. (To Director) I think "Goldilocks" would make a charming story, don't you? The story of the little girl with golden hair. Oh, didn't you just wish you had hair like Goldilocks when you were young? Just like my little girl's? (Looks surprised) Why, isn't that a coincidence? My little girl's hair is the exact shade that Goldilocks had. Oh, you remember my daughter, Pampered Volunteer, don't you? Say hello to the director, Pampered.

PAMPERED
No. I want to go get an ice cream cone.

VERONICA
You'll have to excuse her. She's just excited about being back on the stage. You remember last year she played the Butterfly Queen in the Spring Sing? I happen to have a few pictures here of her in her costume. (She whips out a wallet and flings open the photo section which is about a foot long.) Oh, here she is in her cocoon and here she is dancing to "Be My Little Baby Bumble Bee". Isn't she precious? And here is her father's favorite and over here...

DIRECTOR
That's very interesting, Veronica, but I have a lot of work to do before all the kids arrive. Perhaps you could help me by organizing these audition cards and...

VERONICA

Help? Oh, darling, I am sorry. I would love to help you, of course, but I have a Save The Whales Meeting at noon and a charity tea at two and, well, it is Tuesday and I have a standing appointment with Mr. Irving for my hair...I'm afraid I just came to drop by Pampered, although the very idea of her auditioning is laughable. Now, Pampered, stop biting your nails and you do what the lovely director says, all right?

PAMPERED

I want an ice cream cone.

VERONICA

She's going through a p-h-a-s-e right now. But I am sure you can make her bloom into the star she should be. Oh, look at that time, I must be off. Kiss-Kiss, Pampered. Kiss-Kiss to you too, darling. Order me four seats for opening night. Ta ta. (SHE EXITS)

DIRECTOR

Well, Pampered, it looks like you and me against the world. I am sure you're going to be a big help for me and...

PAMPERED

I want an ice cream cone...I want an ice cream cone...

DIRECTOR

Well, it looks like ME against the world. Pampered, would you do me a favor and open the auditorium doors? I think we have a group of young actors and actresses who are anxious to audition for our show. (Pampered doesn't move.) Okay, okay. I'll get you an ice cream cone.

PAMPERED

With sprinkles?

DIRECTOR

With sprinkles. (Under her breath) I wonder if Steven Spielberg has this much trouble.

(Pampered goes to the door and opens it. **ALL GROUPS ENTER.** If music is used, have the children enter singing a big musical number about the wonders of show biz and how great it is to be in a show. There are a lot of songs like this out there or you could have someone write one for you. If music is not used, have them come in with controlled noise. They do not have to get up on the stage but can stand in the aisles looking up at **DIRECTOR**. This should be a pretty big group as it includes everyone in the entire play.)

DIRECTOR

Now, quiet down, please...Please quiet down. (They do) Thank you. Now I am excited so many of you are here to audition for our play. I've chosen the script which is called "A Salute To The Five Basic Food Groups" and...

(The children all groan)

ERNIE

The Food Groups again? I wanted to do "The Phantom Of The Opera".

CINDIE

I wanted to do Cinderella.

CARL

I wanted to do "Long Day's Journey Into Night".

FREDDIE

I wanted to do "Nightmare On Elm Street, Part Seventeen".

DIRECTOR

"Nightmare On Elm Street"?

FREDDIE

Yeah, you know with a lot of dead bodies and a hack saw and...

DIRECTOR

Why don't you stand over there, young man. Thank you. Now, calm down...Calm down. We'll all do different things once we see what kind of talent you have. I can adapt the script to fit all of these ideas.

FREDDIE

All right.

DIRECTOR

Well, almost all...Now, how many of you have been in plays before. (No one raises their hand, except for **PAMPERED**.)

DIRECTOR

Yes, dear, I know about you. None of you have had any theatrical experience? Well, that makes two of us. Now go off to your classrooms and wait. I will call you when I need to see you. (They go off singing again, if possible. **MINDROT ENTERS**...She is a teenager with spiked out hair and very punky.)

MINDROT

Hey, like are you the director of this thing?

DIRECTOR

Yes, are you here to audition?

MINDROT

Get real. I'm here to help you. I'm your assistant director.

DIRECTOR
Oh, did the principal send you?

MINDROT
No, my parole officer. I have to do fifteen hours of community service so here I am. Like, what is this place?

DIRECTOR
We're putting on a play and I will need all the help I can get. What's your name?

MINDROT
It's Mindrot.

DIRECTOR
Mindrot? I can't call you that. What's your first name?

MINDROT
Scuzzy.

DIRECTOR
I'll call you Mindrot. Okay, let's get the first group out here and see them audition. Would you call Miss Thompson's class, Mindrot?

MINDROT
Sure. (Goes to edge of stage and yells off.) Hey, you little rug-rats, get out here on the double!

DIRECTOR
Mindrot, I could have done that.

MINDROT
Then, why did you have me do it? Sheesh.

(**GROUP ONE MOVES TO THE STAGE** from the aisles. These groups can be any size from a small group or solo act to a full class. They should have suggested costumes for the number they will do. The other groups quietly file backstage.)

DIRECTOR
Okay, kids. Let me see the audition number you've been rehearsing.

ANDREA
Miss Director, I have a question.

DIRECTOR
Yes, dear.

ANDREA

What's our motivation?

DIRECTOR

What?

ANDREA

I mean, what is our intrinsic motivation vital to our capturing the essence of our characterization?

DIRECTOR

(Putting her arm around the child.) Your motivation is you do it because I'm the director, that's your motivation. Got it?

ANDREA

It's kinda like being a mom, huh?

DIRECTOR

Right. Now do it.

(**GROUP ONE** does any musical number they can do here.)

DIRECTOR

That was wonderful! You guys are definitely in the show.

(**THEY ALL CHEER**)

DIRECTOR

Report to the wardrobe lady for fittings. Off the stage now. I want to see the next group. (**GROUP ONE EXITS**)

MINDROT

You want me to go round them up?

DIRECTOR

No, thanks, Mindrot. I think they can find their way.

(**GROUP TWO MOVES TO THE STAGE**)

DIRECTOR

Okay, now I want to see plenty of energy on this number. I hear that your teacher has been really working you hard to learn this number. I bet she really wants to see you in this show. She must be very proud of you.

ROBBY
Are you kidding us? She just wanted us out of the class for an hour a day for rehearsal.

CARLA
(With all sweetness...) We're incorrigibles, aren't we kids?

(They all agree with her.)

MINDROT
Hey, my kinda group.

DIRECTOR
You mean the only reason you're auditioning is so your teacher can get an hour off?

GERRI
Yeah. We're your responsibility for an hour.

DIRECTOR
Great. So, what talent do you have?

LOUISE
Well, we can drive a substitute teacher to hysteria in five minutes.

GERRI
And we can make a lot of noise.

(They all start yelling. **DIRECTOR** tries to get them to calm down, but can't.)

MINDROT
Hey, teach, this is my specialty. (Blows a police whistle and the kids get quiet.) Look, you little loud mouths, we're putting on a show here so I don't want any of your lip, understand? Now the first one who acts up, gets a knuckle sandwich. Got it?

(They all nod, terrified.)

MINDROT
You just got to know how to speak their language, teach.

DIRECTOR
Thank you, Mindrot, I think. Okay, now let me see the number you practiced.

(**GROUP TWO** does a musical number. This could be a rock and roll or some "tough" song since they are suppose to be the bad kids. But keep it light.)

DIRECTOR
Very good. We will use that in the show...if you promise to behave. (**MINDROT** makes a threatening gesture to them behind Director's back.)

ALL

Yes, yes we will.

DIRECTOR

Okay, then off you go (THEY EXIT) See, all you have to do is know how to talk to them.

MINDROT

That's for sure.

DIRECTOR

Okay, Mindrot. Who's next?

(COACH SMITH ENTERS with several BASKETBALL PLAYERS)

COACH

Hold it. Hold it just one little old second. What is going on here?

DIRECTOR

We're having auditions for the school's play.

COACH

Not in my auditorium, you're not. I'm Coach Smith and everyone knows this is my time to use the auditorium for a little practice.

DIRECTOR

You practice basketball in here?

COACH

Yep. I have it on the master calendar. Every Monday, Wednesday and Friday, my team and I shoot a few hoops. You probably remember me from my college days? "Hoops" Smith? Almost All State 1972?

DIRECTOR

(Searching through her clipboard) Sorry. I don't recall you. Monday, Wednesday and Friday you say? Well, I suppose I could have rehearsals on Tuesdays and Thursdays.

COACH

No can do. That's when Miss Shinsplints has the Drill Team in here.

DIRECTOR

What about Saturdays?

COACH

That's the time the school's debating team comes in.

DIRECTOR
Sunday?

COACH
Soccer.

DIRECTOR
What about before school?

COACH
The band practices. Hey, why do you think they call it a multipurpose room?

DIRECTOR
Well, Scoop...

COACH
That's "Hoop". Hoop Smith. Almost All State.

DIRECTOR
Yes, well, how about if you let me use it a couple of days a week?

COACH
No can do. My team needs their practice.

DIRECTOR
How about if we put them in the show?

COACH
In the show? My team? On the stage? The bright lights? The glamour? My team up there on stage?

DIRECTOR
That is, if they have any talent.

COACH
Why, sure they have talent. Number 33 over there has a terrific jump shot.

DIRECTOR
I was hoping for something a little more theatrical.

COACH
Huddle, guys. (They go into the huddle and then come out.)

COACH
Okay, you want talent, you got talent. Hit it, Maestro!

(THE BASKETBALL PLAYERS SING A SONG: This could be a harmony type number or any sporting type song. Or they could do a funny version of the school fight song. It could also be a choreographed basketball number done to "Sweet Georgia Brown" like the Globetrotters. This is a great place for a really bad act that is funny. Perhaps the Coach takes the lead and makes a foot of himself. The sillier the better.)

COACH
So what do you think? Are we in the show?

DIRECTOR
Do I get my rehearsal space?

COACH
You got it.

DIRECTOR
Welcome to show biz, Coach.

COACH
All right. Come on, team. We gotta practice. This is our big break. (They run off. Mindrot watches them.)

MINDROT
You really going to use them?

DIRECTOR
Do I have a choice? All right, let's see what else we have here? Mindrot, would you check with the kids back there? They're being too quiet. I'm suppose to meet with the one parent who volunteered to help make scenery.

MINDROT
Okay. I'll keep them quiet. (She starts off and then returns to pick up a catcher's mask.) You can't be too careful. (She exits as the DIRECTOR checks her clipboard as MR. SAWHORSE enters.)

DIRECTOR
Oh, you must be Mr. Sawhorse. Did you have problems finding the place?

MR. SAWHORSE
No problem.

DIRECTOR
Well, I appreciate your volunteering to make our sets for us.

SAWHORSE

No problem.

DIRECTOR

I've made some preliminary sketches here. (She gives him a huge sheet of paper.) I thought I would start with a huge staircase, you know. About forty feet high. I want each step to light up as the children descend it. Then, as they reach the bottom, I want a castle to roll in from stage right and then a magic carpet fly overhead. And during the big finale number, I need about seventeen chandeliers and, oh, yes, a mountain made of spun glass that will erupt chocolate lava during the candyland number. Do you think you could build all that in two weeks?

SAWHORSE

No problem...

DIRECTOR

Oh, that's wonderful Mr. Sawhorse. Will it be ready for our dress rehearsal?

SAWHORSE

No problem.

DIRECTOR

Oh, thank you. It is so nice to have one concerned parent to volunteer for us. The tools and wood are back there. And thank you again.

SAWHORSE

No problem. (He exits.)

DIRECTOR

All right, let's get the next group out here.

(GROUP THREE MOVES TO CENTER STAGE)

DIRECTOR

Okay, let's see the kind of thing you can do for the second act close, okay?

(GROUP THREE CAN DO ANY NUMBER HERE)

DIRECTOR

Terrific kids. And I want to thank you for being so quiet while waiting your turn.

GABE

It wasn't hard. We were awfully busy.

DIRECTOR

What were you doing back there?

CHAN
We were doing an experiment to see which bathroom would fill up with water the quickest.

TODD
The boy's won!

DIRECTOR
Mindrot! Get a mop! Now I want you all to go back there and clean up that mess. Why would you do such a thing?

CHAN
We are torn between a desire to create and a desire to destroy. Besides, there is no one watching us back there.

DIRECTOR
Go clean it up, now.

(THEY EXIT as MR. SAWHORSE ENTERS and starts measuring the stage.)

DIRECTOR
Oh, Mr. Sawhorse. How are the sets coming?

SAWHORSE
No problem. No problem.

DIRECTOR
Oh, I forgot to mention that for the salute to Alaska number I will need a huge iceberg for seventy dancing penguins on it. And I've changed my mind. I really don't need the glass mountain. Instead, could you make an exact replica of an 1876 steam locomotive in one-eighth scale with a working engine and a red caboose?

SAWHORSE
No problem.

DIRECTOR
Mr. Sawhorse, you're wonderful. (Mr. Sawhorse leaves.)

DIRECTOR
Okay, we have time to see the dance number. Are you ready?

(DANCERS ENTER AND DO THEIR DANCE. This can be a solo or group. At end, they all run off as MR. SAWHORSE ENTERS and moves some lumber across center stage.)

DIRECTOR
How's it going, Mr. Sawhorse?

SAWHORSE
No problems. (He exits to back center stage and stays in view working on the set as **MINDROT** passes him.)

MINDROT
What is old man Sawhorse doing here?

DIRECTOR
He's going to help us. Isn't that wonderful?

MINDROT
Yeah, I guess. But I don't know how much good he can do. He doesn't understand English.

DIRECTOR
What? Mr. Sawhorse? Mr. Sawhorse?

SAWHORSE
No problem.

DIRECTOR
Do you understand English?

SAWHORSE
No problem.

DIRECTOR
Oh, thank heavens. For a moment I thought you couldn't understand me.

SAWHORSE
No problem.

DIRECTOR
Mr. Sawhorse, you do speak English, don't you?

SAWHORSE
No problem.

DIRECTOR
Mr. Sawhorse, how do you spell "dog"?

SAWHORSE

No problem.

DIRECTOR

I'm ruined. (She thinks) Wait a minute. I took french in high school. And my sister knows Spanish. Oh, and the principal speaks Chinese. Maybe we can work something out. What language does Mr. Sawhorse speak?

MINDROT

Lithuanian.

DIRECTOR

So, who needs scenery? (She looks at him and gives him the pages.) Please, Mr. Sawhorse. Just follow the instructions. Please.

SAWHORSE

No problem.

DIRECTOR

Okay, get my mind off this. Do we have any of the costumes ready to look at?

MINDROT

(Checking clipboard) Yes. The home ec class has been sewing for the last few weeks.

DIRECTOR

Well, let's see them.

(MUSICAL NUMBER: This can be a fashion show of a serious kind, showing off fashions either donated by local merchants or done by home ec classes, or it can be outrageous costumes left over from other shows, if they are available, or a series of costumes from a rental shop. There should be musical accompaniment and there can be a commentator like a real fashion show.)

DIRECTOR

Well, at least we have costumes. I just hope nothing happens to them. Make sure they hang up their costumes and don't let them run around in them.

MINDROT

Don't worry. I had them hang them up in the bathrooms.

DIRECTOR

Good and...What? That bathrooms? But I thought they were flooded with water. Go check and see if they are okay.

(MINDROT RUNS OUT)

DIRECTOR
That's all I need. No costumes.

(**MINDROT** runs in)

MINDROT
Don't worry, boss. I got them all out.

DIRECTOR
Are they all right?

MINDROT
Oh, sure. They just got a little wet. But they are fine. See. (Holds up an infant's outfit.) I guess they shrunk.

DIRECTOR
Oh, great. Now we have no costumes. What next? I have to relax. I can't take it anymore. I need some peace and quiet. (She sits down)

(**LENORE** pokes her head in)

LENORE
We're ready to do our number now, Director.

DIRECTOR
Is it a quiet number?

LENORE
Oh, yes. It's very soothing.

DIRECTOR
Fine. I need something to soothe my nerves. Go ahead while I have my breakdown in peace and quiet.

(**LENORE** leads her group on.)

(**MUSICAL NUMBER:** This can be a comic number using percussion instruments like pot covers and drums. It should be very noisy.)

DIRECTOR
Thank you, children. That was loud...I mean, wonderful.

LENORE
It's even better when Leon is here. He plays the tuba.

DIRECTOR
I'm sure, dear. Now run along, back to your classroom. Quietly, quietly.

(VERONICA VOLUNTEER enters)

VERONICA
Well, how is it going? Are we making theatrical magic here yet?

DIRECTOR
Veronica, I don't think the sets will be ready on time, the costumes have shrunk, the lighting people never showed up, I have no makeup and the programs have been locked in my uncle's car trunk. I just don't know what's going to happen.

VERONICA
Now, darling, I am sure things will be wonderful. And if they are not...Well, you can always move to a new community. I've told all my friends about it. You can't disappoint the Wednesday Afternoon Literary Tea and Bowling Society. After all, my name is on the program as one of the committee members.

DIRECTOR
It is? Then maybe you'd help us with...

VERONICA
Oh, darling, don't be absurd. I'm only the honorary chairperson of the subcommittee for the advisory board's alternative membership and sunshine group. I don't do work. Well, I'm sure it will be a smash, darling. We're all looking forward to it. Ta ta for now.

(She wafts off. Director sits hopelessly.)

DIRECTOR
That's it. I'm through. I can't do this. It's crazy. I'm just going to have to quit. That's all there is to it.

MINDROT
You going to let Miss Snootyface win? Come on. We can put on a great show.

DIRECTOR
Without costumes? Without sets?

MINDROT
We can do it. With a little imagination and magic. That's what theatre is all about, isn't it? Imagination and magic.

DIRECTOR
But the scenery...The costumes...

MINDROT
It's all part of the illusion of theatre. If you have enthusiasm, the audience will fill in the gaps. And, if there is one thing that our kids have, it is imagination. Can't you just imagine them out there, singing for their folks? Just think about it.

(FROM OFF STAGE, a whistle blows and the lights change to go brighter. The music starts and the **ENTIRE CAST** marches down the aisles onto the stage or in front of the stage singing another Show Bizzy song. They wear bright costumes or hats, singing their hearts out. If possible, the curtain behind them should open up and reveal a very glittery set with stars and balloons. Mr. Sawhorse is seen standing there with his hammer and smiling. The music builds and should have a big ending with the Director center stage and the smallest member of the cast running up with a dozen roses for her. It is indeed the grandest show ever.

CURTAIN OR BLACKOUT

THE END

THE PIED PIPER

PRODUCTION NOTES

This is a fun script since you can use as many rats and villagers as you wish. The rats could be another teacher's responsibility, if you wish, and they could learn a dance or two before they rehearse with the rest of the cast. There is a strong use of music in just having the piper's music heard. You can use tape recordings or, if you are lucky enough to find someone who can play the flute or recorder, grab them. They can play off stage while the piper mimes. The classical piece "Hall Of The Mountain King" by Grieg is a very spooky number.

You also have the option of having a scene in the magic mountain, if you wish, for the purpose of presenting another musical number. There is no dialogue in this optional scene and it can be cut quite easily.

There are several speaking parts of townspeople and mice. They can be combined if you don't have enough kids, or you can divide the lines up to even more. Howard's lines should remain his, but the rest are pretty interchangeable. You can use the younger grades to be the children of the town and have them skip out and off the stage with little rehearsal. You may want to put them into the first scene as well as bystanders. They don't have any dialogue.

SETTING
The play takes place in a village so you can have a background of houses painted. (See illustrations at the bottom of page 23.) (Houses and stores painted on butcher paper and hung from the curtains work fine. Likewise, cardboard cut-outs standing up.) This can be more elaborate, if you wish, since it does not move (unless you show the inside of the mountain). This play is perfect for those who don't have stages with curtains, etc., since there is only the one set.

COSTUMES
Medieval type of costumes are nice. But again, this is a fairy tale and the best bet is putting the boys in brightly colored sweatpants and tunics and the girls in mom's old prom dresses. You can make some cone hats for the girls and attach "silk" hankies to them to make it look more medieval. The mice could be in a dark pajama pattern with mouse ears attached to their heads or in black tights and leotards. Keep their faces visible so mom and pop can get a photo and know which one little Leonard was.

MUSIC
There are places for dances and such which can be cut, but it is fun to watch the mice come out dancing a simple step. Try using some mysterious tunes for the piper's songs and some evil sounding music for the rat's dance. As mentioned before, the classical piece, "Hall Of The Mountain King", by Grieg, is a very spooky number.

CAST LIST

MAJOR DIALOGUE
- Mayor
- Piper
- Dirk

MODERATE DIALOGUE (MICE)
- Morty
- Leon
- Stanley
- Mickey
- Marie

MODERATE DIALOGUE (TOWNSPEOPLE)
- Beatrice
- Prunilla
- Gwendolyn
- Harvey
- Howard
- Maudie
- Glenda
- Phillip

NO DIALOGUE
- Children
- Extra Mice

THE PIED PIPER

---------------------------- SCENE ONE ----------------------------

THE TOWNSQUARE

As the curtain opens, there is no one on stage. Quiet music can be played to indicate a beautiful spring morning. Suddenly, from off stage there is a scream. **BEATRICE RUNS IN.**

BEATRICE
Rats! There are rats in my pantry.

(**PRUNILLA RUNS IN**)

PRUNILLA
Beatrice, what is wrong?

BEATRICE
There are rats in my house. Big ugly grey rats.

PRUNILLA
How awful.

(There is another scream and **GWENDOLYN AND HARVEY RUN IN.**)

GWENDOLYN
There are big rats hiding in our barn.

HARVEY
And they are in my shop. Big ugly grey rats.

(There is another scream. **MAUDIE AND HOWARD RUN IN.**)

HOWARD
There are mice in my cellar.

MAUDIE
Those are rats, Howard.

HOWARD
Great big ugly grey mice.

MAUDIE
Rats, Howard. Those are rats.

PRUNILLA

There are rats in Beatrice's pantry also.

HARVEY

And in my shop.

GWENDOLYN

And in my barn.

ALL

Big, ugly grey rats.

(More screams as **OTHER TOWNSPEOPLE RUN IN.**)

GLENDA

There are ugly grey creatures in my house.

HOWARD

They must be mice.

MAUDIE

Rats, Howard. Rats.

PHILLIP

What should we do?

MAUDIE

Let us ask the Mayor. He will know.

GLENDA

Go ahead and knock, Howard.

HOWARD

What should I say? I never spoke to the mayor before.

PHILLIP

Just tell him our troubles.

(Howard knocks on the door. The door is opened by a gigantic rat. Howard doesn't notice.)

HOWARD

Mr. Mayor, something must be done about the...(He does a double take.) Hey, you're not the Mayor. (The rat giggles and runs off. The **MAYOR RUNS IN EXCITEDLY.**)

MAYOR

Gracious, there are rats everywhere.

TOWNSPEOPLE

We know. We know.

GLENDA

Look out, here come some more.

(The Townspeople hide as the **RATS ENTER**. If you wish, they could do a dance here. It could be a modern dance number about frightening people or a happy number about eating food. At the end, they get together and talk. They sound like gangsters and could be dressed in spats and derbys, smoking cigars.)

MORTY MOUSE

Did you see them run?

LEON

Just like Stanley did when the farmer's wife came after him with the carving knife.

(Stanley turns around and shows he has no tail.)

STANLEY

That's a night I'll never forget. My poor tail.

MICKEY

This town is fun. You were right, Leon. If we unionized, this town would be on it's knees.

LEON

You see? Stick with me. After all, I am the big cheese.

RATS

Cheese? Mmmmmmmm

MARIE MOUSE

But what about all the traps the townspeople will put out?

LEON

What about them? They haven't built a better mousetrap yet. As long as we stick together, we won't have to squeak by anymore. (Talking like Edward G. Robinson.) That is, as long as you guys ain't no dirty rats.

MICKEY

Well, this town may be okay for you little rats, but someday, I hope to go to Hollywood and become a big star.

MARIE

Oh, Mickey. You're always saying that. Why don't you just marry Minnie and settle down?

MICKEY

I'll show you. Someday, my name will be up there in lights. (Gesturing.) Mickey Rat.

LEON

Maybe you should change your name.

MORTY

Come on, gang. The bakery is open. Let's go down and get some cheese danish.

ALL

Cheese? Mmmmmmmm.

(They run off as the **TOWNSPEOPLE SNEAK BACK IN.**)

HOWARD

Are they gone?

PRUNILLA

They're headed for the bakery.

MAYOR

Oh, woe is me. What can we do?

BEATRICE

Yes, Mr. Mayor. What can we do?

(Music is heard way off and the **PIED PIPER ENTERS BLOWING HIS PIPES.**)

MAUDIE

What beautiful music.

GLENDA

I feel like dancing.

HOWARD

It certainly does sound happy.

MAYOR

And we could use some happiness now. Why, look. It's that man playing. (They go over to the piper.) Hello, sir. What happy music you are playing.

PIPER

Allow me to introduce myself. I am the piper. I go from town to town spreading joy and happiness with my pipe.

PHILLIP

How happy!

PIPER

It is! I know how to turn woe into wonderful. Mire into mirth and turn a frown upside down.

TOWNSPEOPLE

How wonderful!

MAYOR

Yes, but music cannot help us now. We are plagued by a huge problem.

HOWARD

Mice.

MAUDIE

Rats, Howard. Rats.

HOWARD

Yes, rats.

PIPER

Indeed?

MAYOR

Yes, our town has become infested with them. We don't know how to get rid of them.

PIPER

Have you tried traps?

ALL

Yes.

PIPER

Snares?

ALL

Yes.

PIPER

Cheetos?

ALL

Yes.

PIPER

Music?

ALL

No?

PIPER

Don't you know that music has charm to soothe the savage rat?

HOWARD

Mice, too?

ALL

Howard!

PIPER

Why, I can rid your town of the rats just like that. (Snaps his fingers.)

ALL

You can?

MAYOR

How?

PIPER

With my pipes. I will charm them off into yon river. (Points off.)

MAYOR

Why, how did you know that was the name of that river?

PIPER

What river?

MAYOR

The Yon River. Named after our founder, Marcellus Yon.

PIPER

Just a lucky guess.

ALL

Can you really do it?

PIPER

I can try.

MAYOR

Do and we will give you anything. Anything.

PRUNILLA

(Aside) Except money. That man is sooo cheap.

PIPER

I will rid the rats for you...

ALL

Hooray!

PIPER

...For a price.

MAYOR

What sort of price?

PIPER

Forty gold pieces.

MAYOR

But, sir, that is more than our entire budget allows.

PIPER

Well, then, I must be off. If it is not worth it to you, you should not pay it. (He starts off.) Oh, excuse me, but whoever owns that cart of hay...

PHILLIP

Yes?

PIPER

The rats have just eaten it.

PHILLIP

Oh, Mayor, pay him, please pay him.

MAYOR

It is too much.

PIPER

Goodbye. (HE STARTS OFF.)

GLENDA

But we cannot live with those rats.

MAYOR

He looks like a simple fellow. Perhaps I can trick him. Piper. Piper, come back. (PIPER TURNS.) We have agreed that if you get rid of all the rats, you shall be paid...(Thinks)...handsomely.

PIPER

Forty pieces of gold?

MAYOR

A job well done gets well paid. (They shake hands.)

PIPER

Then I shall play for the rats. (He begins playing. Music is heard.)

HARVEY

I don't hear anything.

PIPER

That's because you are not a rat. Only rats hear this tune. (The **RATS STICK THEIR NOSES OUT.**)

LEON

What a catchy little ditty.

MICKEY

May I have this dance, Marie?

MARIE

Certainly.

(They all come out and do a dance. At the end of the dance, the **PIPER LEADS THEM** down into the audience and out the back doors of the auditorium.)

PRUNILLA

Look, they are all going down towards the river.

TOWNSPERSON

The rats are jumping into the water.

MAYOR

The piper is getting rid of the rats.

ALL

We are saved. Hooray!

(**THE PIPER REENTERS.**)

MAYOR

It is indeed a miracle.

HOWARD

He has saved us from all those mice.

PIPER

Rats, Howard. Those were rats.

HOWARD

Oh, yes.

PRUNILLA

Let us get back to work now that there are no rats to worry about. (The **TOWNSPEOPLE EXIT** except for the **MAYOR** and **PIPER**.)

PIPER

I have done my job as we agreed. Now for the payment. (He holds out his hand. The Mayor shakes it.)

MAYOR

And you shall have it. Our hearty thanks. (He starts off.)

PIPER

Mayor, are you forgetting? The money?

MAYOR

But we never agreed on a sum, now did we?

PIPER

But...

MAYOR

I just said, "a job well done gets well paid". And you shall. All the ale and bread you can eat at the tavern for, shall we say, twenty percent off?

PIPER

That was not the agreement.

MAYOR

Why squabble over a few paltry cents. The job is done so we don't need you anymore. Thank you, Piper. You saved us from rats and, more importantly, you saved our treasury. (**MAYOR EXITS** laughing. The Piper watches him go.)

PIPER

We'll see about that. I have taken from you what you hated most. Now I shall take what you love most. Your children.

(He starts to play another tune and the **CHILDREN COME OUT**, followed by their parents.)

GLENDA

Jenny, stop!

PHILLIP

Louie, come back here! What's wrong?

HARVEY

It's as if they were bewitched. They cannot stop dancing.

GWENDOLYN

It's the Piper. He has enchanted them.

(The **CHILDREN AND PIPER GO OFF THE STAGE** and into the back of the auditorium.)

PHILLIP

Where are they headed? (They all look out over the audience's heads.)

MAYOR

To Yonder Mountain. Next to Yon River.

TOWNSPERSON

But what does the Piper want with our children?

BEATRICE

Look, the mountain is opening up. The children are skipping inside it. (There is the sound of great rumbling.)

BEATRICE

All except for Dirk, the orphan boy. He cannot keep up with them.

MAYOR

Now the mountain is closing. Our children are gone. All gone.

(**DIRK ENTERS** from the back of the auditorium.)

MAYOR

You, young man, what happened to our children?

DIRK

The Piper brought them to a wondrous place. I wish I could have gone with them.

MAYOR

But surely you know something else. Something that will help us get our children back.

GLENDA

What was this magic place like, Dirk?

DIRK

It was a beautiful land, Mayor. Where promises are kept and money owed paid. Everyone was happy and there was honesty and love everywhere.

HOWARD

Unlike SOME places we know about.

BEATRICE

Yes, Mr. Mayor. Because of your cheapness, we may never see our children again.

(The **CURTAIN FALLS** on the sad group.)

BLACKOUT

---------------------------- SCENE TWO (OPTIONAL) ------------------------

This can be eliminated if you do not wish to change sets. Otherwise, it can be done in front or the curtain with just suggested sets. There should be giant lollipops and gingerbread cutouts (see above illustration) and the children could enter with the Piper and do a dance or sing a song about their happy land. There doesn't need to be any dialogue.

------------------------------ SCENE THREE -------------------------------

THE TOWNSQUARE
All the people are sitting listlessly about.

BEATRICE
I do miss the children.

HOWARD
It has been six weeks since they have gone.

MAUDIE

It is the Mayor's fault. He cheated the Piper and made us lose our children.

MAYOR

But people, think of the money I saved you.

PHILLIP

What good is money without the joy of our children to spend it on?

GLENDA

Money cannot buy their smiles.

PRUNILLA

Or their laughter.

MAUDIE

Or their hugs.

(They all start to cry.)

MAYOR

You are right. I did a terrible thing. Oh, if only I could reason with the Piper.

(The **PIPER APPEARS.**)

ALL

Look! He has returned.

MAYOR

Piper, I am glad to see you. Please, you must return our children. We will give you anything you wish.

ALL

Yes, please return our children.

PIPER

I see you have learned your lesson. If you want to dance, the Piper must be paid.

MAYOR

You are right. I am sorry to have cheated you. Here is the gold. (Hands him a sack from his belt.) And more than you requested. Only, please forgive me and return our children.

PIPER

(Counting out the money.) I only want what is due to me. My forty pieces of gold. You now know, Mr. Mayor, that cheaters never prosper.

MAYOR
I do.

(**DIRK ENTERS** and sees the Piper.)

DIRK
Oh, Piper. Please take me with you to join the others in that magical land.

PIPER
I am afraid that is impossible, Dirk. That land is the land of dreams. We can visit it for a short time only, but no one can live there. It is a place where promises are kept and no lies are told.

DIRK
You mean, I shall never live in such a land?

PIPER
You might, but only if everyone agrees to live good honest lives and to always be truthful and honest.

ALL
We'll change. Honest.

PIPER
Then let us bring the land of enchantment here. Let your children return from Yonder Mountain...

MAYOR
You know its name also?

PIPER
Let the children lead you to a world of truth and honesty.

(**HE PLAYS HIS PIPERS** and the **CHILDREN RUN IN.**)

BEATRICE
Look, here comes Becky.

MAYOR
And Tommy and Sally.

GLENDA
And my little Wally.

(The parents hug their children.)

ALL

Thank you, Piper. Thank you.

MAYOR

And from now on, we shall be truthful and honest as the children have shown us.

HOWARD

I haven't been this happy since we got rid of all the mice.

ALL

Rats, Howard. Rats!

(They all laugh and the Piper plays a merry tune and they dance.)

CURTAIN

THE END

THE EMPEROR'S NEW CLOTHES

PRODUCTION NOTES

Kids love this play because there are so many funny characters. And the idea of being onstage in one's underwear is almost as much fun! There are plenty of chances for music and dancing in here, if you wish. And you can add as many characters as townspeople as you wish.

SETTING
A townsquare is the major set. (See illustration above.) This can be as elaborate as you wish since the other scene in the castle can be done downstage with just a screen or in front of the curtain. All you need for the second scene is a coat rack and some hangers. Dick and Dack can be either sex and I have seen this done as "The Empress's New Clothes" with the same success.

COSTUMES
A note about the underwear scene. Make sure that the underwear the Emperor wears is funny and loud and covers up the child playing the part. Don't expect a little boy to be comfortable walking out in his real briefs and no shirt. Have him wear brightly colored long johns or some other elaborate type underwear that no one could possibly mistake as (gasp) REAL underwear. The louder they are, the funnier the bit is.

The townspeople costumes are rags (easy job here) and the court costumes are standard King and Queen issue (that is, a cardboard crown and a cape). Dick and Dack can wear loud eccentric clothes. Videl should be the height of fashion. Don't be afraid of being a bit anachronistic here. Kids will readily identify if Videl is wearing the latest in "rad" rags.

CAST LIST

MAJOR DIALOGUE
    Emperor Ego
    Videl Baboon
    Empress Elaina
    Dick
    Dack

MODERATE DIALOGUE (TOWNSPEOPLE)
    Ernie
    Mother
    Louisa
    Aunt Ess
    Fred
    Charlene
    Lisa
    Charles

NO DIALOGUE
    Extra Townspeople

THE EMPEROR'S NEW CLOTHES

--------------------------------- SCENE ONE ---------------------------------

THE TOWNSQUARE

There are houses and stores. The townspeople are rushing about working hard, mending and sewing great bundles of clothes. They are dressed in rags. They could sing a song about their hard life.

ERNIE
Mother, I am so tired.

MOTHER
Quiet child. We have work to do.

LOUISA
But, mother. All we do is work, work, work.

AUNT ESS

Hush, now. Don't let the Emperor's guards hear you complain.

ERNIE

Yes, Aunt Ess.

FRED

The children are right. We work too hard.

LISA

All we do is mend and sew and wash and take care of the Emperor's clothes.

AUNT ESS

And why not? He has the only closet in the Kingdom stuffed with beautiful things.

FRED

The rest of us must wear rags.

LISA

Oh, for the days before the Fashion Consultant arrived. Remember how kind and loving the Emperor used to be?

MOTHER

But those days are gone for good. Since the sneaky Fashion Consultant came, all the Emperor thinks about is...

ALL

Clothes, clothes, clothes.

LISA

Hurry, now. Back to work. We still have lots of work to do.

ERNIE

I have to wash sixty five pairs of socks.

LOUISA

And I have to press fifty pairs of pants.

MOTHER

And I must sew buttons on his royal shirts. All sixty eight of them.

AUNT ESS

Hurry, hurry.

(They all get back to work as **DICK AND DACK ENTER**.)

DICK
What a strange town.

DACK
I have never seen people work so hard.

DICK
It looks like an excellent place for us to sell our Cure-All.

DACK
Yes. Let's set up. (They put their suitcase on a stand and open it. They take out a banner that reads "Dr. Proctor's Cure-All For Sale".

DICK
Hurry, hurry, hurry. Step right up here. For only one crown, we have the best Cure-All in the Kingdow.

DACK
Guaranteed to cure warts, blisters, bad breath, dandruff and whooping cough. Step right up. Step right up.

(Everyone continues to work.)

DICK
Dack, what is wrong with these suckers...I mean, customers?

DACK
These people seem too busy to stop and shop. Sir? (Tries to stop someone.) Sir? Why do you not stop and shop with us.?

CHARLES
I have no time. I must shine all sixty-four pairs of the Emperor's shoes.

DACK
But why?

CHARLES
We all work to keep the Emperor's clothes looking nice. It is the rule of the Kingdom.

DICK
The Emperor has so many clothes that an entire village must work on their upkeep?

CHARLES
Oh, this is just his everyday clothes. Tomorrow, we will be working on his formal wear. He loves clothes.

DACK
He sounds very vain to me.

AUNT ESS
Quiet. Don't let the Fashion Consultant hear your complaints or you will be beheaded.

DACK
But why do you all dress in rags as you clean his clothes?

AUNT ESS
We have no money for our own clothes. It all goes to taxes so the Emperor can have new clothes.

DICK
What? I have never heard of such a thing. I should like to meet this man.

MOTHER
He will be here soon. He comes to bring us his dirty laundry. He doesn't trust the guards to bring it down.

ERNIE
Here comes the Emperor now.

MOTHER
(Looking off.) Oh, and the Fashion Consultant is with him. Hurry, everyone. We must get the work done. (They all scurry off except DICK AND DACK WHO STAND BACK and watch as EMPEROR EGO, EMPRESS ELAINA AND VIDEL BABOON ENTER.)

EMPEROR EGO
What were you saying, Videl?

VIDEL BABOON
I said, Your Grace, that plaids are out this year. Now the big fashion statement is tweeds. And, mid calf, of course.

EMPEROR EGO
Of course.

EMPRESS ELAINA
But, Ego, you've just spent the national treasury on putting the hemline above the knees.

EMPEROR EGO
But now, they must be mid-calf, correct, Videl?

VIDEL BABOON
If one wishes to remain fashionable, yes, Your Grace.

EMPEROR EGO
You see, dear. No one knows fashion like Videl Baboon.

EMPRESS ELAINA
Yes, dear. (She sighs.)

DICK
(Whispering) That Videl guy is just making a baboon out of the Emperor.

DACK
It takes a con man to see a con man. He's a phoney.

VIDEL BABOON
For a mere thousand crowns, Your Grace, I can see that all the work is done to your specifications to have the hemline at the correct length.

EMPEROR EGO
Yes, yes, of course. It will mean a tax increase, but it shall be worth it. The peasants would certainly want me to be fashionable.

DICK
We must do something.

EMPEROR EGO
(Spotting them.) Say, why aren't you two working? I have shoes to be polished and stockings to be darned.

DICK
Your Grace, we are not of this Kingdom.

DACK
We are from the land of Sir Calvin The Kline.

DICK
We bring you greetings from him.

EMPEROR EGO
Sir Calvin The Kline? The fashion plate of the western kingdoms?

DICK
That is correct. We bring you news. The latest fashion news.

VIDEL BABOON
How can you? Only I know the latest fashion news.

DICK
But this is newer news. The latest thing from the continent.

DACK
Suits made of unicorn horns and butterfly wings.

EMPEROR EGO
Sounds beautiful.

EMPRESS ELAINA
Sounds costly.

VIDEL BABOON
Sounds phoney.

DACK
This suit is made of the most beautiful and lightest of materials.

DICK
You shall be the envy of all who see it.

DACK
And a special price for you, sire, since you are in the fashion business.

EMPEROR EGO
I must have it. I must.

VIDEL BABOON
But sire, you know nothing about these roustabouts. Perhaps they are thieves.

EMPEROR EGO
Nonsense. They speak of fashion. Of course they must know the latest news. You are invited to my castle to make such a suit for me.

DICK
With pleasure, Your Grace.

EMPEROR EGO
Now, come along. I can't wait to be the height of fashion.

(DICK AND DACK SHAKE HANDS as the curtain falls.)

BLACKOUT

------------------------------ SCENE TWO ------------------------------

THE ROYAL SEWING ROOM
(This can be played before the curtain.) There is a screen and a table with fabric on it. Perhaps a fitting dummy is there. A full length mirror may also be there. **DICK AND DACK ARE SEATED,** lazily playing cards.

DICK
I say, Dack, we have been in this sewing room for over three days. Don't you think we should let the Emperor see something?

DACK
But what? We don't know how to sew.

DICK
But there must be a way to help those people out.

DACK
I told you, as soon as we get the money, we'll give it to the townspeople. But we have to get an idea first.

(There is a knock at the door. **DICK AND DACK JUMP UP** and grab the material, pretending to sew.)

DICK
Go away. We are busy.

(VIDEL BABOON ENTERS.)

VIDEL BABOON
It is Videl Baboon, Royal Fashion Consultant to the stars. Hard at work, I see. Or is it "hardly working"? I don't see any designs yet. Perhaps you are in bigger trouble than you thought.

DACK
What? You don't see our design? YOU the fashion consultant don't recognize a doublet made of Moonbeams and Fantasies?

VIDEL BABOON

What? Where?

DACK

The doublet. Right here. (Holds up an empty hanger.) You know, the wizard who sold us the material said it had magical powers. He said that only wise men could see it...Ridiculous, isn't it?

VIDEL BABOON

Ridiculous?

DICK

Yes. Imagine. Saying that only people who really understood fashion could see something that is as plain as the nose on your face.

DACK

Imagine someone not being able to see this beautiful shade of blue and gold along the collar of this vest. (Holds up another hanger.)

DICK

Oh, it is beautiful, isn't it?

VIDEL BABOON

Beautiful? (He tries to touch it.)

DACK

The wizard told us only fools cannot see the truth. And this cape is woven with the fibers of Truth and Light.

VIDEL BABOON

What?

DICK

We know you can see it. After all, you are the Fashion Consultant. But we worry some of the fools in the village could not...

DACK

Not knowing what real fashion is.

VIDEL BABOON

Yes, well you know those fools. They couldn't see the nose in front of their own faces.

DACK

But you do, don't you?

VIDEL BABOON

Of course. Anyone can tell the doublet is the most beautiful I've seen.

DICK

That's the vest.

VIDEL BABOON

Oh, yes. Of course.

(There is a knock at the door and EMPRESS ELAINA ENTERS.)

DICK & DACK

Your Majesty.

EMPRESS ELAINA

I stopped by to see how the work was going, gentlemen.

VIDEL BABOON

MiLady, look at these beautiful garments that these men have made for your husband.

DACK

They are woven with truth and light.

EMPRESS ELAINA

I should very much like to see them.

DICK

They are right in front of you, your highness.

EMPRESS ELAINA

What?

DICK

Only a FOOL cannot see the truth. Do you not understand, Your Grace?

EMPRESS ELAINA

"Only fools can't..." (She understands.) Why, what a pity. They miss out on such beautiful things. I love them. I just love them.

DACK

We thought you would.

EMPRESS ELAINA

I cannot wait for my husband to see them.

(EMPEROR EGO ENTERS in robes.)

EMPEROR EGO
So, this is where everyone vanished to. Sneaking a peek at my newest outfit. Is it done, tailors?

DICK
(Pretending to sew a hem.) Just finishing off the hem now, sire. (Bites off invisible thread.) There. (Holds it up.) How do you like it?

EMPEROR EGO
Like what?

DICK
The suit. Is it not beautiful?

VIDEL BABOON
What style.

EMPRESS ELAINA
What color.

EMPEROR EGO
What are you talking about?

EMPRESS ELAINA
And to think that fools cannot see these beautiful threads.

EMPEROR EGO
What's that?

DICK
Only a fool cannot see the truth, Your Grace. They are made of magic materials. Can you imagine someone foolish enough not to be able to see these clothes?

EMPEROR EGO
(Not sure.) Yes...I mean...No. I mean...Only a fool, you say?

DACK
That is right.

EMPEROR EGO
And Videl, you see the royal robes?

VIDEL BABOON

Oh, yes, Your Grace. In fact, I was wondering if these tailors might not make me new robes as well. Oh, nothing like yours, sire, but I do love their work.

EMPEROR EGO

Yes, of course. It is...unusual?

DACK

And worth the price.

EMPEROR EGO

Yes. Yes of course it is.

DACK

It is a shame that the townspeople will not see such a beautiful wardrobe.

EMPEROR EGO

I know. I shall proclaim tomorrow "National Admire The Emperor's New Wardrobe Day" and my subjects will be allowed...(Thinks about it.)...Oh, five minutes from their work to admire my new clothes.

EMPRESS ELAINA

How wonderful.

EMPEROR EGO

It is a treat they will long remember.

DICK

Oh, no doubt about that, Your Grace.

DACK

No doubt that we shall all remember such a day.

(They admire the clothes as Dick and Dack laugh.)

BLACKOUT

------------------------------ SCENE THREE ------------------------------

THE TOWNSQUARE

AUNT ESS

Oh, I am so excited about seeing the new clothes.

FRED
Remember what the page said. Only fools cannot see the clothes.

LISA
Then I shall see wonderfully for I am not a fool.

MOTHER
Nor I.

LISA
But what if I do not see anything, Mother?

MOTHER
Hush. Then pretend to see it. You don't want anyone to think you don't understand high fashion, do you?

LISA
No, mama.

CHARLES
Look! Here comes the Emperor now.

FRED
What color is his new robes? It is too far to see.

AUNT ESS
Let me get my specs on. I don't want to miss this.

ERNIE
Oh, this is so exciting.

(DICK AND DACK ENTER.)

DICK
Loyal subjects of Emperor Ego. It is with great pleasure that we show you the Emperor's newest addition to his wardrobe, made available through your generous gifts of taxes.

DACK
This robe is so beautiful, so lovely and so light that the truth surely shows through.

DICK
Presenting Emperor Ego's new clothes.

(They all bow as **EMPRESS ELAINA AND VIDEL BABOON ENTER.** They march past the townspeople and **EMPEROR EGO ENTERS** in a pair of long red underwear. The townspeople gasp.)

LISA
Uh...Lovely, Your Grace. Just lovely...I think.

CHARLIE
I have never seen anything like it.

AUNT ESS
I don't see...(All look at her shocked.)...How you've gotten by without one before, Your Majesty.

MOTHER
It must be comfortable in the summer, Your Highness.

EMPEROR EGO
I knew you would like it.

VIDEL BABOON
Look at the cape and the way the vest fits just so.

EMPRESS ELAINA
And the watch fob is made out of solid gold.

EMPEROR EGO
I look magnificent, do I not?

ALL
Yes, Your Grace.

ERNIE
But, mother, the Emperor is in his underwear.

(ALL GASP.)

MOTHER
Excuse him, Your Grace. He is a child and does not understand fashion like we do.

VIDEL BABOON
The child is a fool.

DICK

No he is not. (Takes Ernie out of the crowd.) It is you who are all fools. The Emperor *is* in his underwear.

ALL

What?

EMPEROR EGO

You lied to me?

DACK

No sire. The robes *are* made of truth like we said and it exposes the Emperor as being the fool that he is.

EMPEROR EGO

How dare you...(He looks down and realizes he is in his underwear. He hides behind Empress Elaina.)

DICK

Anyone who doesn't live his own life like he wants is a fool.

DACK

You have to follow what you think is correct, not what someone else says is in fashion or the cool thing to do.

DICK

If you don't follow your own dreams and goals, you may end up like the Emperor, embarrassed to be in his underwear in the town square.

EMPEROR EGO

Elaina, take me home. I'm mortified.

VIDEL BABOON

I told you this would happen, sire. You should have worn your velvet breeches with the gold inlay...

EMPEROR EGO

Oh, be quiet, Videl. You're fired!

VIDEL BABOON

What?

EMPEROR EGO
I shouldn't have listened to you in the first place. All that talk about fashion and glamor. And just look at me now. Instead of helping my people out, I spent all the time looking at fashion books. That was wrong. So, Videl, get out of my Kingdom and take your trends and fashions with you.

VIDEL BABOON
Well, I never...How will you know what's in style, then?

EMPEROR EGO
I shall listen to my heart to learn what is right for me. Now, go!

VIDEL BABOON
Very well. I am glad to get out of this Kingdom. It wouldn't know a fashion statement if it bit it. (As he goes) By the way, Your Majesty, that hair style went out with baby blue buckles. (Storms off.)

(ALL LAUGH.)

EMPEROR EGO
Thank you, Dick and Dack for showing me what a fool I have been.

DICK
You are more than welcome, Your Grace.

EMPEROR EGO
And here is the salary I owe you for this suit.

DACK
Keep it, sire. Let it pay for the people's new clothes.

EMPEROR EGO
Right. Except this time, we'll make sure we can see them.

(ALL DANCE as curtain falls.)

THE END

RED RIDINGHOOD'S ADVENTURE

PRODUCTION NOTES

Again, this is pretty easy to stage. You can add as many children as you wish at the beginning and end as well as dances and music as you wish. You can also divide up Woofie Wolf's part into several wolves or just have the pack out there with Woofie and Waldo.

SETTING

This can be tricky since there are three sets. The first one can just be the suggestion of a house (a front porch leading off). Or, if you are really clever, one side of a flat can be the exterior of Red's house while the other side, when turned, shows Gramma's house. Don't worry about doors. Have the kids walk around it and pretend there are doors there. One side would have the outside of the house and the other have a sampler ("Home Sweet Home") and a window with lace curtains all painted on. (See illustrations above.) Then add a bed and perhaps a table in front of it to suggest Grannie's pad. You don't have to use a real bed here. You can cut out the foot of a bed from plywood or cardboard and stand it upright, so when the wolf gets into bed, he is actually standing behind it.

The scene in the forest requires no set and can be played in front of the curtain. If no curtain is available, have a couple of trees in the first scene and then just remove Red's house and voila! You're in the woods. Bring Grannie's house on for Scene Three (leaving the trees for background) and you've managed to do the set changes.

COSTUMES

Don't cover the wolf's head with a mask. Remember, the wolf has a mom and dad who want to take pictures for Granma. A furry body and a set of pointy ears attached to a cap will suffice. The wolf should not be scary.

It's pretty obvious that you are stuck in getting a red cape for you-know-who. Not terribly difficult, but let the kid have a couple of days rehearsal with it to get used to it. You'll be amazed what set pieces she can find to snag it on if you give it to her five minutes before curtain. Granny wears a long nightgown and the hunter is dressed in jeans and a flannel shirt. The children wear everyday clothes.

CAST LIST

MAJOR DIALOGUE
- Nikki - Little Red Ridinghood
- Waldo Wolfington
- Grannie
- Mother
- Woofie

MODERATE DIALOGUE
- Hunter
- Vernon
- Christie
- Cindy
- Jenny
- Billy
- Tommy

NO DIALOGUE
- Children
- Extra Wolves, if desired

RED RIDINGHOOD'S ADVENTURE

--------------------------------- SCENE ONE ---------------------------------

Nikki's front yard. The house is stage left with a small picket fence around it. There are trees in the background. As the curtain rises, Vernon and the children could be singing a song and doing a dance. If not, they could run in and start calling to the house.

VERNON

Nikki! Nikki!

CINDY

Maybe she isn't home.

(**NIKKI ENTERS** wearing a red cape.)

NIKKI

What is it, Vernon?

VERNON

Come on. We're going to play some games.

NIKKI

I don't think I want to play. I may soil my new red cape.

JENNY

Gee, Nikki. You never do anything anymore since you got that riding hood. You're always afraid you'll get it dirty.

VERNON

Why not take it off and come play with us?

NIKKI

Oh, no. It is so beautiful that I am never going to take it off. Ever.

CHRISTIE

Then you're never going to play with us?

NIKKI

Oh, Vernon, we've always played together. But now, I have my red cloak and don't need to play with anyone. I can just run through the fields and let the sun shimmer on it. Look how it billows when the breeze rustles through it.

TOMMY

Oh, Nikki. Everyone knows you have the cape. We're all tired of you showing it off. The townsfolk are even beginning to call you names.

NIKKI

What sort of names?

BILLY

Some people are beginning to call you "Little Red Ridinghood" because no one sees you without your hood on.

NIKKI

Little Red Ridinghood? What a happy name. I like it.

VERNON

Please come and play with us, Nikki. We miss you.

NIKKI

I can't play now. I have to wash my red hood.

NANCY

But you wash it everyday.

NIKKI

You're just jealous. All of you. You wish you could have a cape like this one to keep you warm. The whole village is jealous, but I don't care. I would rather have this cape than any friends like you.

VERNON

We aren't jealous. But you value that cape more than our friendship. Someday, Little Red Ridinghood, you're going to wish you had friends instead of that silly cape.

NIKKI

Jealous, jealous, jealous.

CHRISTIE

Good-bye, Little Red Ridinghood. I hope you are very happy being so alone.

(THE CHILDREN AND VERNON EXIT.)

NIKKI

(Touching the cape lovingly.) Oh, I do love you, riding hood. You are so pretty. I don't care what the townspeople say. I love you.

(MOTHER ENTERS)

NIKKI

Mother, did you hear the pretty name the villagers have given me? "Little Red Ridinghood". Oh, I must look so pretty in my cape.

MOTHER

Now, Nikki, you look very sweet in your hood, but you must not get vain.

NIKKI

But mother, I am the luckiest girl in the world. The other children are jealous of me.

MOTHER

Perhaps they would not be so jealous if you did not brag so. You must remember that you are a very fortunate little girl to have a grandmother who can sew so beautifully.

NIKKI

I know. Oh, mother, feel how warm the lining is. It's like angel wings.

MOTHER

It is beautiful. But, nevertheless, you will find yourself friendless if you become vain over what you have and others do not.

NIKKI

Yes, mother.

MOTHER

Now are you ready to go to Grandmother's house?

NIKKI

Oh, yes. I love having a chance to wear my new cape. Is she feeling better today?

MOTHER

I think so. The traveling merchant was there yesterday and said her cold is much better. Wait till you see the goodies you are to bring her. (Goes to porch and brings back basket.) Fresh gingerbread, some pumpkin bread and half a dozen chocolate chip cookies. I am sure they will make her feel better. They are her favorite kind.

NIKKI

Mine too.

MOTHER

But no tasting on your way to Granny's house. I wish I were going with you, but I promised your father I would have the roast goose done tonight for dinner.

NIKKI

I'll be careful, Mama.

MOTHER

The woods are dark and damp, so don't go talking to strangers.

NIKKI

Don't worry. I'll have my cloak to keep me warm.

MOTHER

Give Grannie my best and I hope to see her soon.

NIKKI
All right, Mama. I'll be good. Bye.

(SHE SKIPS OFF as Mother watches.)

CURTAIN

------------------------------ SCENE TWO --------------------------------

A CLEARING IN THE WOODS. This may be played before the curtain or Nikki's house could be removed to show more of the trees. **WALDO AND WOOFIE ENTER.**

WOOFIE
I tell you, Waldo, the other wolves aren't going to like your running out on them.

WALDO WOLFINGTON
Sorry, Woofie, but that den is so cold, I just can't stand it. (Sneezes) I think I've caught my death of cold.

WOOFIE
Waldo, you are suppose to be a wolf. Mean and fierce. What's the matter with you?

WALDO WOLFINGTON
It's just when I get cold, I don't feel very fierce.

WOOFIE
I told you you shouldn't have shed so much fur last molting season. I'm going back to the meeting. Go home and get some sleep.

WALDO WOLFINGTON
If only I could. But my cave is too damp and cold.

WOOFIE
Good luck, Waldo.

(HE HOWLS AND EXITS.)

WALDO WOLFINGTON
Brrr. I hate winter. This fur isn't enough to keep me warm and I'm always so hungry since there are no apples or vegetables to eat. Oh, why wasn't I a flamingo or some other animal in warmer places? Why did I have to be a wolf.

(NIKKI ENTERS)

NIKKI
Hello. (Waldo jumps)

WALDO WOLFINGTON
What? Oh, you startled me. Hello, little girl. What are you doing way out here in the cold?

NIKKI
I'm on my way to my granny's house. She is ill so I'm bringing her favorite cookies to her. Chocolate chip.

WALDO WOLFINGTON
My favorite as well. (Sneezes)

NIKKI
Bless you. Do you have a cold?

WALDO WOLFINGTON
Yes. It's from sitting in cold caves during pack meetings.

NIKKI
You should have a hood like mine. It keeps me very warm.

WALDO WOLFINGTON
It does look warm. You wouldn't consider trading for it, would you?

NIKKI
Ridiculous. What could a wolf have to trade with?

WALDO WOLFINGTON
Well, there's...And of course my favorite...Uh...I don't suppose you'd consider a bunch of old rocks as a good trade?

NIKKI
For my lovely hood? Of course not. I wear this everywhere. The townspeople call me Little Red Riding Hood and my mother says...Oh.

WALDO WOLFINGTON
What's wrong?

NIKKI
I just remembered that I'm not suppose to talk to strangers.

WALDO WOLFINGTON
Allow me to introduce myself then. I am Waldo P. Wolfington the Third. How do you do?

NIKKI
Fine, thank you.

WALDO WOLFINGTON
Now, you see. We aren't strangers anymore. Now how about letting me try on your cape?

NIKKI
No. I won't let anyone wear my cape.

WALDO WOLFINGTON
But don't you know it's always a good thing to share?

NIKKI
Not my cape. Good-bye, Mr. Wolfington. I have to go now.

(SHE SKIPS OFF)

WALDO WOLFINGTON
Wait! Don't go yet! Can't we talk about this? Drat. (Mutters to himself) I must have that cape. If I don't, I shall freeze to death. Think. Think. (He paces) Aha! I have it. Her granny's house must be the one over the hill. If I go there, I may be able to get that cape. And who knows? Maybe even a few cookies. Now, if I can only remember that shortcut. (He points off) Away, feet. Tonight, I shall be dressed warmly for once.

(HE HOWLS AND RUNS OFF)

BLACKOUT

--------------------------------- SCENE THREE ------------------------------

GRANNIE'S HOUSE
This can be the back side of Nikki's house placed center stage or just with suggested sets. There is a bed and a table.

GRANNIE IS SITTING IN BED, sniffing. **WALDO ENTERS** and stands outside the house. He knocks.

GRANNIE

Goodness gracious, who can that be? Who is it?

WALDO WOLFINGTON

(Outside) It's...(in falsetto) I mean, it's your granddaughter.

GRANNIE

Oh, Nikki. How nice of you to come. Come in. (**WALDO ENTERS**) Wait, you're not Nikki. You're one of those awful wolves.

WALDO WOLFINGTON

Oh, please dear lady. Let me in from out of the cold. I have a message for you from your granddaughter.

GRANNIE

A message from Nikki? What is it?

WALDO WOLFINGTON

Well...Ummm...That is...She says she thinks she left her red cape here last time she visited.

GRANNIE

Her red ridinghood? Piffle. She never takes it off.

WALDO WOLFINGTON

Nevertheless, she says she would like you to look in your closet for it. Just in case she did leave it here.

GRANNIE

Well, all right. I doubt if it's here but I'll look. (She opens an imaginary closet door to off stage and peers in.) I don't see anything.

WALDO WOLFINGTON

Look closer. (He sneaks up behind her and pushes her into the closet and locks it.) Sorry, Grannie, but I must have that cape or freeze. Now, I must hide. (He darts around the room, trying out different hiding places. He spies Grannie's robe and night cap.) Wait! I have an idea. If I dress up like Grannie, the little girl will mistake me for her. When she comes in, I'll have her take off her coat and then grab it and run. Along with the cookies. (He puts on robe and night cap.) There. I look just like Grannie. (Knock at the door is heard. Waldo answers in falsetto.) Just a minute, dearie. (He runs to the bed and put blankets over himself.) Come in. (**NIKKI ENTERS**) Why, granddaughter, how nice of you to visit old Grannie. Do come in, Vickie.

NIKKI

My name is Nikki, Grandmother.

WALDO WOLFINGTON
Oh, yes. Of course. I was thinking of my other granddaughter, Vickie.

NIKKI
But I'm your only granddaughter, Grannie.

WALDO WOLFINGTON
Of course you are. You know Grannie. Always teasing. (Tries to laugh it off.)

NIKKI
How is your cold, Grannie?

WALDO WOLFINGTON
(in regular voice) Cold? What cold?...I mean...(in falsetto) Oh, yes, my cold. Much better thank you. (He takes out a hanky and blows his nose loud and long and very ungramma-ish.) Why don't you relax a bit and take off that lovely jacket?

NIKKI
I'm fine, thank you, Grannie.

WALDO WOLFINGTON
But it is so warm in this house. You'll feel so much better with it off, dear.

NIKKI
Oh, but I love it so much. I never take it off. I brought you some cookies, Grannie.

WALDO WOLFINGTON
Good. (Takes basket and starts eating cookies.) But I really cannot enjoy these until I know you are comfortable. That cloak looks so heavy.

NIKKI
I'm fine, Grannie. Really. (Wolf snaps fingers in distress.) Gracious, Granny, but your cold must have settled in your nose. What a big nose you have.

WALDO WOLFINGTON
It's all swollen up. I can't smell a thing.

NIKKI
Golly, Grandma, I never noticed but what big eyes you have. I hope it's not hereditary.

WALDO WOLFINGTON
Well, they're all puffed up too with this nasty cold. But it's all the better to see your beautiful cape with.

NIKKI

And, Grannie, your mouth seems ever so large.

WALDO WOLFINGTON

The better to eat your delicious cookies with, my child.

NIKKI

And your hands! They are so big.

WALDO WOLFINGTON

(Jumping up and in his own voice.) The better to take your cape away, my dear.

NIKKI

Oh no! You're Waldo Wolfington. Help! Help! (She runs about screaming.)

WALDO WOLFINGTON

I've got you now. Let me have that cape or I'll gobble you up.

NIKKI

Not my cape. Help! (They run about but the wolf finally gets her cornered.)

WALDO WOLFINGTON

There's no one to help you now.

(VERNON, THE HUNTER AND THE CHILDREN ENTER.)

VERNON

You see? I told you I heard screams.

HUNTER

So the wolf is picking on someone smaller again, eh?

WALDO WOLFINGTON

All I wanted was her cape.

NIKKI

Thank goodness you came.

HUNTER

You'll be all right, little girl. As soon as I take this wolf away.

WALDO WOLFINGTON

Away?

HUNTER
Yes. I'm going to take you back to our zoo in California. That way you'll cause no more trouble.

WALDO WOLFINGTON
California? Warm weather? Sun tans? Beaches? Oh, when do we leave? Can I bring my sunglasses? Hang ten. Kowabunga. Let's boogie.

HUNTER
Not until you tell us where Nikki's grandmother is.

WALDO WOLFINGTON
Oh, she's in the closet. I didn't hurt her. (They open the door and Grannie tumbles in.) Now can we go? I can't wait to go to California. Maybe I'll even get my own TV show. (HE DRAGS THE HUNTER OFF.)

NIKKI
Oh, Grandma. Thank heaven you are all right.

GRANNIE
That nasty wolf wanted your cloak.

NIKKI
I know. But thanks to my friends, I'm all right. Vernon and everyone, thank you so much. I guess you were right. Everyone needs friends.

TOMMY
We were glad to do it, little Red...

NIKKI
No, call me Nikki. Now, who wants to try my cloak on?

(They all gather around. It could end with a dance. If not, all the children should be trying on the cloak and laughing.)

BLACKOUT

THE END

THE ENCHANTED BEDPOST

PRODUCTION NOTES

This is a fun and easy-to-produce holiday program in which the entire school can become involved. The casting is simple, with the majority of the lines being said by five or six characters, but with enough for even the youngest actors to get involved.

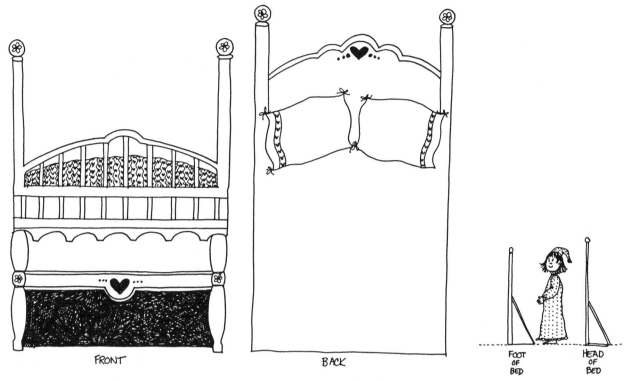

SETTING

The settings can be as simple or as elaborate as you wish. Do not use a real bed for Jody and Jill. Instead, use a cut out of the foot of a bed with bedposts that they can stand behind, making it appear they are in bed. (See illustration above.) This way, if you want, you can slide it off easily when the curtain opens to reveal Santa's Workshop. The Workshop can be as elaborate or as simple as you wish. You can get by with having a large clock with the months of the year hanging on a curtain with several tables filled with brightly wrapped presents. A beautifully decorated Christmas tree can fill up an empty spot nicely as well. (See illustration below.)

Or you can make an entire factory for production, with different departments marked with signs like "Baby Doll Testing Department", "Painting Department", "Wrapping Department", etc. Perhaps an ingenious mom or dad could build a set with a toy making machine that is whirling away at the beginning of the scene.

COSTUMES

Pretty standard stuff here. The children wear pajamas, Santa wears a Santa suit. The elves could be in brightly colored sweatpants with tunic tops and little caps. They should have rosy cheeks and do not worry that some of your elves may be too tall. That's fine. Fantasy comes in all sizes and shapes. The reindeers should wear brown colored costumes (pajama patterns with the little booties attached work great). They wear baking caps with antlers attached. (You can find antler type caps in a lot of novelty shops now, if you want to invest the money, or you can make them out of firm cardboard.) The toy soldiers can wear brightly colored tunics or simply a couple of bands of colored material crisscrossed over the chest and a tall hat, made out of cardboard. The dollies can wear doll clothes, depending on whether you want them to be rag dolls or porcelain dolls. Just remember to make all the costumes colorful and comfortable.

MUSIC

I have included quite a few musical numbers here, simply because a lot of Christmas carols fall in the public domain and can be used easily. Additionally, you may have a talented tune smith in your P.T.A. who may want to try a hand at writing original tunes. You can use a live piano player or use taped music. Again, be creative with your choices. There are some pretty good new carols that come out and several novelty Christmas songs that are not done to death every year. Also, you don't need to stick just to Christmas carols. Use other happy songs. After all, how many times can you listen to "Jingle Bells"?

SPECIAL NOTES

The part of Jody can be a boy or a girl, depending on your casting. It would be nice to have a man and a woman play Santa and Mama Claus, simply because little brothers and sisters who come see the play are always disappointed when a child comes out dressed as Santa. If you want to use a student, find an older one who can at least appear taller than the rest of the cast. (Although, he is a "merry LITTLE elf", I suppose.)

Do not be afraid to incorporate other ethnic holiday numbers. Every nationality has some wonderful songs or customs that can easily be incorporated into the show with the simple addition of an elf running out and announcing that the toys for (name of country) are ready and then have the toys explain what they symbolize to that country. Explanations of other holiday preparations, such as Hanukkah can be incorporated as well, to make this a holiday pageant for all. The holiday season should be for everyone. Don't make anyone feel isolated because they don't celebrate like you do. Ask students for input and then use their ideas.

CAST LIST

MAJOR DIALOGUE
- Jill
- Jody
- Ernie Elf
- Edith Elf
- Santa Claus
- Mama Claus

MODERATE DIALOGUE
- Mother
- Sandman
- Elvira Elf
- Edward Elf
- Esther Elf
- Eugene Elf

SPECIALTY NUMBERS
- Elves
- Reindeers
- Dollies
- Candy Canes
- Wind Up Toys
- Toy Soldiers

THE ENCHANTED BEDPOST

---------------------------------- SCENE ONE ----------------------------------

JILL AND JODY'S BEDROOM

This is played before the curtain. There is a cut out of a bed stage left. The two children sit beside it in their nightgowns as their **MOTHER** reads to them.

MOTHER
...And we heard him exclaim as he drove out of sight, "Merry Christmas to all, and to all a good night."

JILL
Does Santa Claus really live at the North Pole, Mother?

MOTHER
As far as I know. With all his elves, making holiday gifts for everyone.

JODY
And Mrs. Claus too? (Mother nods) Oh, how I would love to meet them all.

MOTHER
Oh, they're a happy bunch, I can tell you that. Especially the elf in charge, Ernie. Why he works so hard, he hardly has time to sneeze.

JILL

Do you know them, Mother?

MOTHER

I visited them once, long ago.

JODY

You went to Santa's Workshop? How?

MOTHER

Oh, it was years ago. In this very room. I was just about your age and the Sandman came and took me off by putting a spell on the bedpost. And faster than you can say Jack Frost, I was there.

JODY

What kind of spell did he put on the bedpost?

MOTHER

Oh, a very special one. One he can only use on Christmas Eve. And he only does it for children who truly believe. It's the only way to get there.

JILL

We believe.

MOTHER

Oh, and there is one more thing.

BOTH

What? What?

MOTHER

You have to be sound asleep.

JODY

But how can we go anywhere when we're asleep?

MOTHER

That's the magic part. Now into your beds and shut your eyes. (The children do as she says.) And wish, very, very hard. Dream of Santa's Workshop. Dream, dream...

(Mother could sing a lullabye here if the director wishes. At the end **SHE BACKS AWAY** as the lights dim a bit.)

JILL

Are you thinking, Jody?

JODY

Uh huh. (They sit up and look around.) But we're still here. Still in our bedroom.

JILL

Maybe this old bedpost isn't enchanted after all.

JODY

Don't say that. Remember we have to believe. Believe.

JILL

Well, all right. I believe. I really, really, really, really do believe.

(There is magical music and from behind the bed, the **SANDMAN APPEARS**.)

SANDMAN

That's better! (The children jump up.) I thought that magic had worn off long ago.

JILL

Who are you?

SANDMAN

Me? Why, I'm the Sandman, of course.

JODY

The Sandman! Have you come to take us to Santa's Workshop to meet Santa Claus?

JILL

And Mrs. Claus?

BOTH

And all the elves?

SANDMAN

Only if you really, really want to.

JILL

We do.

SANDMAN

All right then. Into bed and close your eyes while I use my special sand to get you there.

(He throws out a handful of glitter over them.)

(SONG: A Christmas Carol or any other appropriate song.)

(During the bridge of the number, the lights begin to flash. If no song is used, simply start the lights flashing.)

JILL
What's happening?

JODY
The bed, it's moving. We're going. We're going to The North Pole.

CURTAIN OPENS BEHIND THEM
(The curtain opens up and there is a workshop set.)

------------------------------ SCENE TWO ------------------------------

The **ELVES ARE HARD AT WORK** and join in the song of the Sandman. At the end, Jody and Jill get out of bed and the Sandman takes them to the center of the square.

If there is no curtain, have the elves run out and set up a simple screen with the set designed on it.

The elves sing a happy work song as they make the toys. Jill and Jody watch in amazement. **ERNIE THE ELF RUNS OUT** blowing a whistle.

ERNIE ELF
Hold it everyone, hold it. Hold it. Hooooold it! (The work stops.) We have a catastrophic condition. Look at this. Just look.

ELVIRA Elf
What is it, Ernie?

ERNIE ELF
We are four days behind schedule. Look at the clock. (They look at the clock that reads the months of the year instead of the hours. It moves up to December.) It's December all ready and we're way behind. We still have all those baby dolls to teach to say "Mama", those toy trucks to test drive and we haven't even started on the toys for all the children at (name of local school or town). And you know how good they've been this year.

EDWARD ELF
Except for one or two. (Goes to footlights.) And they know who they are.

ERNIE ELF
So, hurry up, elves. Hurry, hurry, hurry.

(**ALL THE ELVES SCATTER** except for Ernie.)

JODY

Look, Jill, we must be in Santa's Workshop.

(ERNIE spots them.)

ERNIE ELF

What are you two elves doing out of uniform? Don't you know we are behind schedule? Who is your immediate elf supervisor? This is going on your permanent record, I'll have you know.

SANDMAN

They are not elves, Ernie. These are children. Jill and Jody.

ERNIE ELF

Children? Children in Santa's Workshop? (He tries to hide the presents.) What are you doing here?

SANDMAN

They believe so hard, I had to bring them Ernie.

ERNIE ELF

But children aren't allowed in here. Not nohow. Not nowhere.

JILL

Please, Mr. Ernie, we want to see Santa.

JODY

I want to tell him what I want for Christmas.

ERNIE ELF

That's impossible. No one sees the big guy this close to the holidays. You will have to go back home.

SANDMAN

Come along, children. I'm afraid Ernie is right. I shouldn't have brought you here.

(EDITH THE ELF ENTERS)

EDITH ELF

Hello, Ernie. I brought the latest count of letters from the mailroom for your report to Santa. I also made you some cookies. They're your favorite.

ERNIE ELF

(Tongue tied) Oh, hello, Edith. How are you?

EDITH ELF
Fine. Where were you this afternoon? I thought we were going ice skating?

ERNIE ELF
Oh, I had a problem. Someone put the stuffed kitties next to the toy doggies and we had a big fight.

EDITH ELF
Ernie, can't you think of anything but work?

ERNIE ELF
As head elf, I have a lot of responsibilities.

EDITH ELF
(Sighing) Yes, Ernie. I know. I know. (Sees the children) And who are these two?

ERNIE ELF
They're a couple of children who the Sandman brought by. Can you imagine that? Children in Santa's Workshop? Why, they'll throw the entire schedule out of whack. (Looks at watch) Gracious, I'm fifteen point seven seconds behind my rounds. Edith, make sure these two get back home and then go back to the mailroom. I have to get to Quality Control. (**HE RUNS OUT**)

EDITH ELF
Ernie, you forgot your cookies. (Sighs)

JILL
You like him, don't you?

EDITH ELF
Who? Ernie? Well I guess so.

SANDMAN
Now Edith, everyone knows you have your cap set for him. It's all over Wonderland.

EDITH ELF
Well, I guess I do like him...A little. But I work down in the mailroom and he works up here.

JODY
Do you get a lot of letters?

EDITH ELF
Oh, my yes. We're so busy all the time, I hardly get to see my Ernie.

(Optional song here. Could be about love or about working in Santa's mailroom and getting your letters organized. If no song, continue with dialogue.)

JODY
Say, if you're so understaffed, perhaps Jill and I could help. That way, Ernie may have more time for you and think of romance instead of progress reports.

JILL
And we could meet Santa Claus.

SANDMAN
That's a wonderful idea. But we'll have to disguise you. What size elf outfit do you wear?

EDITH ELF
I hope it's small, cause that's all we have. Come along with me. I'll fix you up. But don't tell Ernie. He'll be upset.

(EDITH AND THE CHILDREN EXIT as an excited ERNIE RUNS IN FOLLOWED BY EDWARD ELF.)

ERNIE ELF
Oh goody...We are up production by sixteen percent over last year and we've cut absenteeism by four percent resulting in a flow of 34 percent more toys per capita. Santa will be so proud.

EDWARD ELF
Gee, Ernie. I thought making toys was suppose to be fun.

ERNIE ELF
Fun? Fun? Are you kidding? We have a quota to reach. I didn't spend all that time in school getting my M.B.E. (Aside) That's Masters of Business Elfdom...just to have fun. (Checking his list) Now, Edward, I want to see those new baby dolls...The ones that sing and dance.

EDWARD ELF
Right, boss.

(HE GOES OFF AND WITH A COUPLE OF ELVES BRINGS OUT THE DANCING DOLLS. They could be several girls dressed as dolls with rosy cheeks and baby clothes. They can do any musical number here either about being a doll or a Christmas number. It would be a good place for a ballet number or a rag doll number with a loose limbed doll doing a soft shoe. At the end, Ernie nods approvingly.)

ERNIE ELF
Excellent. Excellent. These will be perfect for some of those children at (name of school).

Except for the few bad ones. (Goes to footlights) And you know who you are.

(JILL AND JODY START IN, crossing the stage. They are dressed in ill fitting elf costumes. They see Ernie and try to run out.)

ERNIE ELF
Hold it, you two. No one is allowed up here while I'm reviewing new toys. (Looks at them) Say, haven't I seen you two before?

JODY
No. We've been working down at the toy drum division.

JILL
Yeah. We're beat. (Laughs at joke) "Beat", get it?

ERNIE ELF
If I didn't know better, I would think you two are...

(ESTHER THE ELF RUNS IN.)

ESTHER ELF
Ernie! There's a problem down in the mechanical toys division.

ERNIE ELF
Problem? What's wrong, Esther?

ESTHER ELF
Look at this work order. The order was for 6,000 one foot toy soldiers. Someone goofed and made one thousand SIX foot soldiers.

ERNIE ELF
Who could have made such a mistake?

ESTHER ELF
I think it was your two new assistants. (Points at Jody and Jill)

JODY
But wait till you see them, Ernie. They're great.

ERNIE ELF
But six feet tall?

(Jody whistles and the MARCH OF THE TOY SOLDIERS BEGINS, with a group coming out in soldier costumes. They do a synchronized movement. AT THE END THEY ALL SALUTE AND EXIT.)

JODY

I think the children will love them.

ERNIE ELF

But they're not on my list.

JILL

Maybe you should forget your list and enjoy Christmas.

ERNIE ELF

Don't be silly, it's my nervous breakdown and I am enjoying it. But I want you two out of the toy department. I'm assigning you to Mrs. Claus' Candy Kitchen to help make the Christmas cookies. But if there is one more mishap, you'll be out on your pointy little ears. Understand?

JODY

Yes sir.

ERNIE ELF

Edward, take these elves to the Candy Kitchen. And no more mess ups.

EDWARD ELF

Right boss. Come along.

(**EDWARD, JODY AND JILL EXIT** as Ernie consults his chart. There could be an optional elf number here with the elves all working hard to make toys. If not, dialogue continues.)

ERNIE ELF

Hurry up, everyone. Hurry up. We have lots to do. (**A GROUP OF ELVES RUN BY** with toys. Each one presents a toy for inspection. As they do, **EDITH ELF ENTERS** and joins the end of the line.) Very good, Edgar. (The next one holds up a toy.) Looks great, Edwin. (The last one holds up a toy.) That will do nicely, Ellen. To the wrapping department, quickly.

(**THE ELVES EXIT** as Edith holds a sprig of mistletoe over her head.)

ERNIE ELF

Edith, what is that?

EDITH ELF

I thought you might want to test out the mistletoe. (Puckering) Does it give you any ideas?

(He thinks and then brightly adds:)

ERNIE ELF
Yes it does. I have to check the windup toys.

EDITH ELF
Oh, Ernie.

(SHE STOMPS OFF)

ERNIE ELF
What's bothering her? (Shrugs) Let me see those new windup toys, fellas.

(A GROUP ENTERS AS STUFFED ANIMALS. Ernie goes to each one with a giant key and pretends to start them up. They could be a band of animals with musical instruments and during the number, they keep running down. It could be done to recorded music with the music getting slower until Ernie runs around and starts winding them up. As soon as he gets one going, another starts going down and he is soon running ragged to keep it going.)

ERNIE ELF
Okay. This batch will do well. Off to Santa's sleigh with you.

(THEY ALL START OFF as Ernie goes back to his work. One little stuffed animal stays on, tired by it all and falls asleep. Ernie turns and sees her. He winds her up and she runs off. Ernie laughs as **JILL AND JODY ENTER** in baking hats and aprons.)

ERNIE ELF
Hold it, you two. Where do you think you're going?

JILL
We wanted to see some of the new toys Santa is making.

ERNIE ELF
I thought you two were assigned to the kitchen to help Mrs. Claus bake cookies.

JODY
We were, but we got someone to help us down there.

ERNIE ELF
(Checking his list) You did? But who? Everyone has been assigned another job. Who in the North Pole did you get to help bake cookies?

JILL
Just seven of the best helpers around. Look.

(She whistles and the **REINDEERS COME OUT.** They are dressed in brown with antlers coming out of their baking hats. Rudolph has a very red nose. They carry trays of cookies and candy canes. They can do any Christmas number or songs about the reindeers here or a song about cooking. It should be a funny number with them dancing around, pretending to make cookies.)

ERNIE ELF

Reindeers in the baking department? Cookies all over the workplace? This will never do. (Blows whistle) Get out of here, you antlered cookie makers.

(THE REINDEERS EXIT WITH JILL AND JODY.)

ERNIE ELF

Now, where did those two elves go?

(Looks around and **EDITH ENTERS**.)

EDITH ELF

Is there anything wrong, Ernie?

ERNIE ELF

Oh, it's those new elves. They seem to be doing everything wrong. I swear they probably never even went to Elf Training School.

EDITH ELF

Now, Ernie, just relax. You've been working too hard. You have to just take things easy.

(Optional song here about enjoying life and all the happy things in life. If not, continue with dialogue.)

ERNIE ELF

That's all very easy to say, but someone has to be responsible for getting all the toys together.

EDITH ELF

But I'm sure Santa doesn't want you to give up everything just for your work.

(She sits down next to him and they get very close.)

ERNIE ELF

Well, maybe I could relax, for a moment or two.

(They are just about to kiss when **EUGENE ELF RUNS IN**.)

EUGENE ELF

He's coming. He's coming. Santa Claus is coming.

(Ernie jumps up.)

ERNIE ELF

Santa Claus? Coming now? Oh, there's so much to do. Everyone, places. Places. The chief is coming.

(ALL THE ELVES RUN IN and do a number about Santa Claus. During the number, SANTA CLAUS AND MAMA CLAUS ENTER. At the end of the number, the elves can either run off or stay, sitting in the background.)

SANTA CLAUS
Merry Christmas, everyone. Merry Christmas.

ERNIE ELF
Merry Christmas, boss.

SANTA CLAUS
Well, Ernie, how is everything going?

ERNIE ELF
Fine, chief. Just fine. Production is up, unemployment down, and I have the new flow charts explaining how by merging the bicycle department with the stuffed animal division, we can diversify the two departments and...

SANTA CLAUS
Whoa, there, Ernie. I just wanted to know how you were. I didn't expect a stock holders meeting.

ERNIE ELF
But, Santa, I want to show you the new quotas I've been working on.

(They look at a chart as Mrs. Claus and Edith meet downstage.)

MAMA CLAUS
Oh, Edith, how are things going in the romance department?

EDITH ELF
Horrible, Mrs. Claus. Maybe if I were a toy, he'd notice me.

MAMA CLAUS
Don't you give up hope. We'll think of something.

SANTA CLAUS
That's all fine and good, Ernie. But I've come to look over my new toys. What have you got to show me?

ERNIE ELF
Oh, Santa, I think you're going to like this one. It's the Candy Cane Choir.

(THE SINGING GROUP ENTERS dressed in red and white striped costumes. They can sing any carol here. At the end, THEY EXIT.)

SANTA CLAUS

Wonderful. Such sweet harmony.

MAMA CLAUS

They were lovely, Ernie.

(From behind a stack of boxes, there is a sneeze.)

SANTA CLAUS

Gracious, who is that?

(**JODY AND JILL ENTER** from behind the boxes.)

JODY

It was us, Santa.

ERNIE ELF

Oh, it's those pesky new elves. I thought I told you two to get back to work.

JODY

But...But...

MAMA CLAUS

Wait a minute, Ernie. (Goes to them and takes off their caps.) These two aren't elves. They're children.

ERNIE ELF

Children? In Santa's Workshop? Why that's unheard of.

SANTA CLAUS

Now, calm down, Ernie. Tell me children, what are you doing here?

JODY

We heard that you were understaffed and we wanted to help out.

JILL

So Ernie would have more time to spend with Edith.

ERNIE ELF

You mean you did all this so that I could spend more time with Edith?

EDITH ELF

That's right, Ernie. They were helping me.

ERNIE ELF

Why, I'm speechless. No one has ever wanted to help me out before.

SANTA CLAUS

You see, Ernie. Christmas isn't a time for flow charts and projection tables. It's the small things, like helping a friend.

(Optional song here about the wonders of Christmas.)

SANTA CLAUS

So you see, Ernie, Jody and Jill were trying to help you by giving you the best gift of all...Not all presents come in big brightly colored boxes you know. They wanted to give you the greatest gift of all...The gift of time. Perhaps you should put that time to good use.

ERNIE ELF

But I still have fifteen thousand basketballs to try and thirty thousand bugles to test and...(They all look at him. He slowly tears up his flow charts and takes Edith's hand.)

ERNIE ELF

You're right, Santa. Christmas is a time to be with those you love. Edith, would you like to go for a walk tonight? According to the North Pole weather report, it's going to be a lovely 50 degrees below zero.

EDITH ELF

Oh, wonderful, Ernie. I'll bring a picnic.

ERNIE ELF

At the North Pole? Why, cold cuts, of course. (They all laugh.)

SANTA CLAUS

You children have shown the greatest Christmas spirit by giving your friends some helping hands. I don't know how to thank you.

MAMA CLAUS

Perhaps a special treat like one of my candy canes. (She presents them with a large candy cane.)

JILL

Thank you, Santa. But I'm afraid we have to be getting back home soon. We've been up awfully late. (She yawns)

JODY

Yes. We want to make sure we're home for Christmas morning. (He yawns)

JILL

Besides, mommy must be really worried about us.

SANTA CLAUS

Very well. (Calls off) Sandman. Come forward.

(SANDMAN ENTERS)

SANDMAN

Yes, Santa?

SANTA CLAUS

Looks like we have a couple of sleepy heads here. Perhaps you could help them get back home.

SANDMAN

Of course.

SANTA CLAUS

Good-bye children. And thank you for helping us.

JILL AND JODY

Good-bye Santa, and everyone.

ERNIE ELF

And thank you for showing me that Christmas is more than just a time to work. It's a wonderful time of the year.

EDITH ELF

Come and visit us again soon.

(The Sandman leads them to their bed downstage.)

SANDMAN

Off you go.

(Optional lullabye number here with the entire cast coming out to sing. The children get into bed and fall asleep. If no song is used, have the cast come out and wave good-bye to the children. The curtain slowly falls behind the bed. Jody wakes up when the curtain is closed.)

-------------------------------- SCENE THREE --------------------------------

THE BEDROOM

(Jody wakes up with a start.)

JODY

Jill! Jill! Wake up. We're back home.

(Jill wakes up)

JILL

But where is Ernie and Edith and Santa and Mrs. Claus?

JODY

Maybe it was all a dream.

(Jill holds up the candy cane Mrs. Claus gave to them.)

JILL

Or was it?

(They look at each other as...)

BLACKOUT

THE END

FREE CATALOG !

Send for **FREE** catalog of INNOVATIVE CURRICULUM GUIDEBOOKS AND MATERIALS in Movement Education, Special Education and Perceptual-Motor Development.

Write:

FRONT ROW EXPERIENCE
540 Discovery Bay Blvd.
Byron, California 94514

Questions? Call 415-634-5710